WHAT EVERY NEW COMMUNITY COLLEGE STUDENT NEEDS TO KNOW

Wayne Silver
Three Rivers Community/Technical College

KENDALL/HUNT PUBLISHING COMPANY
4050 Westmark Drive   Dubuque, Iowa 52002

CONTENTS

ACKNOWLEDGMENTS

I owe thanks to many colleagues who reviewed a summary of the book and made helpful suggestions: Alfred Carter; John Coggins; Carolyn Curtis; Jonathan Daube; Booker De Vaughn; John Fisher; Aida Garcia; Nicholas Gennett; Harvey Irlen; Carol Kuozubski; Kathy Kinane; Susan Kinick; Gail Mellow; Frances Moulder; Bobbi Ossip; John Perch; Elaine Pelliccio; Mary Posner; Barbara Segal; William Schwab; Lee Thornton; Peter Walsh; John Whitman; and Dianne Williams.

As always, I am grateful to Emely for her wisdom, insight and unflagging support.

— Chapter 1 —

YOU'VE MADE A
WISE DECISION

As a new student in a community college, you could be:

✓ eighteen years of age, thirty, fifty or over eighty;
✓ African American, White, Latino, Native American, Asian American or none of these;
✓ a lifelong or longtime resident of the United States, a new arrival or a citizen of another country;
✓ single or married, with or without children;
✓ a recent high school graduate or someone returning to school after many years;
✓ a full-time student or, like many others, a part-time student with a job and family responsibilities;
✓ one of many members of your family to attend college or the first.

You may have decided to enroll a while ago or on the spur of the moment, perhaps as a result of a job layoff, a divorce or some other unexpected event. Possibly, you have a firm goal, like transferring to a university or starting a new career, but you also may be confused and searching for direction. In short, you could be anyone.

But one thing is certain. Whoever you are and whatever your reasons for attending a community college, you have made an excellent decision. Like nearly half of all college students in America, you have come to the conclusion that a community

1

college is the most convenient and affordable route to higher education.

As a new student, however, you may not know all of the benefits of a community college education. This chapter introduces you to seven major benefits of the community college experience. You've probably considered some of them, but others will surprise you.

The First Benefit: Excellent Preparation for Transfer to a University

Since many community college students want to transfer to a university when they complete the associate degree, it is important for community colleges to prepare their students well. Fortunately, they do. A 1992 study conducted at the University of Michigan at Ann Arbor found that students who went to a community college first and then to a four year college were just as likely to graduate as their counterparts who began studying in a four year college right after high school. A similar study conducted last year by the California Postsecondary Education Commission revealed that students who went first to a community college did as well or better academically as their counterparts at a four year college or university. A recent study in Arizona illustrated a similar pattern and also demonstrated that African American, Latino and Native American transfer students from community colleges did better academically than their peers who began at a four year college or university.

In commenting on the Arizona study and many others, Professor Richard C. Richardson of the School of Education at Arizona State University concluded, " The issue is not if [community college] transfer students do well; we know that they do."

So if you are planning to transfer to a university after you complete your associate degree, you can count on being well prepared for that transition.

2

The Second Benefit: Increased Income and Career Flexibility

Some community college students do not intend to transfer to a university. Their goal is to complete an associate degree or occupational certificate program, find a good job and increase their earnings. Fortunately, a community college education leads to that result. According to Don Doucette and John Roueche, Professors of Education at the University of Texas at Austin, "associate degree recipients earn 29 percent more than those with only a high school education. Black associate degree recipients earn 51 percent more than those with only a high school diploma; women with an associate degree earn 40 percent more than those with only high school."

The obvious way that a community college education leads to higher income is by preparing students for new careers. Even in a tight job market, people who complete an associate degree have a good chance of finding employment in their chosen fields. Doucette and Roueche note that associate degree recipients may need to wait a while after graduation, but most of them eventually find jobs related to their academic programs.

Another way that a community college education leads to higher income is by making people more valuable to their present employers. As students acquire new abilities and greater self confidence, they increase their job security and likelihood of promotion. This is one of the benefits of a community college education that occurs at every stage of the process, not just at the end.

Finally, a community college education prepares an individual for a broader range of jobs. Many employers are willing to train someone if the person is able to read and write well, perform essential mathematical tasks, use a computer, speak and listen clearly, solve problems and work effectively with others. Associate degree recipients are qualified for a surprising number of jobs outside of their fields simply because they possess the general abilities employers want.

So if you are enrolling in a community college to increase your income and career options, you have made a wise decision.

The Third Benefit: Learning to Navigate in a Complex, Rapidly Changing Society

Our society is changing at a dizzying pace. Daily, we confront new technological advances, new questions and new problems. One day we read or hear about the "integrated information appliance," which will combine a computer, a fax, a picture phone and a duplicator in one unit. The next day, we learn of astonishing medical breakthroughs that could allow us to create artificial blood, transplant brain cells and use fetal tissue in the treatment of disease.

Can any of us keep up with it all? Of course not. However, your community college education will help you ask the right questions, think critically about the answers you receive and find additional information when you need it.

It will also start you on an educational journey that will never end. Like others, you will need continuing education and training throughout your life. That is the only way you will be able to adapt to constant changes in the workplace and the rest of society. Marvin J. Cetron, President of Forecasting International, predicts that by the year 2000, most Americans will spend 32 hours a week working, with the remainder of their time devoted to further education and preparation for future job related challenges.

So think of your community college experience as the first step in a lifelong process of education. As you will see from the rest of this chapter, the process has many personal as well as professional rewards.

The Fourth Benefit: Involvement in a College Community

Many new students think of community colleges as "commuter colleges," places where people attend classes and immediately return home or to work. Nothing could be further from the truth. The typical community college offers a wealth of activities beyond the classroom. Whatever your interests, you are likely to find a way of becoming involved.

Each college is different, but almost all sponsor activities and organizations in the following areas:

Cultural, civic, and educational activities. As a small sample, a recent edition of the college newspaper at Three Rivers Community Technical College in Norwich, Connecticut, announced these events: a performance by the Second Step Players, a regional comedy troupe which educates the public about mental health and illness; the College Spring Artsfest, a full month of plays, musical performances, art displays, dance and mime performances and book, poetry and dramatic readings; a college/community seminar on the merits of the President's Health Care Plan; a one-man performance of "Can I Speak For You, Brother," a powerful play focusing on African American history and culture; a college sponsored speech contest; a gathering to view the solar eclipse of May 10, 1994; a display of computer-assisted designs; a Technical Quiz Bowl; a Children's Book Festival; a lecture/discussion on the multi-cultural society; and a wheelchair basketball game that rounded out a series of programs on people with disabilities.

Sports and fitness activities. Many community colleges sponsor competitive sports teams for men and women, and virtually all offer intramural sports activities for those who want to participate. Some schools also have fitness centers or cooperative agreements with fitness centers in the area.

Social and recreational activities. Throughout the year, community colleges hold dances, picnics, foodfests, hikes and other activities that let people relax, make friends and enjoy themselves.

Community projects and volunteer activities. Community colleges offer many opportunities for community involvement. Students everywhere are participating in Habitat for Humanity projects, holding food drives for local soup kitchens, helping in homeless shelters, performing in nursing homes, reading books to small children and tutoring older ones.

Clubs and interest groups. Community colleges sponsor numerous student organizations and encourage students to start new ones. Some of the groups are primarily social, while others are built on a shared interest or concern, such as environmental awareness, Latino culture, parent-child relationships, poetry or the joys of cave exploration.

Organizations with a professional focus. Some student organizations emphasize the academic or career interests of students. These groups offer relevant programs and try to create valuable relationships between students and local professionals. For example, an accounting club might sponsor a mentorship program through which students work with and receive the guidance of an accountant in the community.

Student publications and performing arts activities. Community colleges vary, but most have student run publications, including college newspapers, yearbooks, magazines and special interest journals or newsletters. They also provide numerous opportunities for participation in plays, musical productions, speech contests, art festivals, poetry readings and other performance activities. Many of the students who involve themselves in student publications or the performing arts have no prior experience with these activities. You don't need to be a veteran to take part, just willing to learn and try something new.

Student government and college decision-making. Community colleges include their students in decision-making at many levels. In addition to a student government, most commu-

6

nity colleges recruit student representatives for college-wide councils, committees and task forces.

At this point, you may be saying to yourself that these activities sound worthwhile, but you'll never be able to fit them into a hectic schedule of classes, work and home responsibilities. That's a normal but self defeating reaction. Even the busiest students find ways to participate in college activities. Look for opportunities consistent with your schedule. You'll learn a great deal, meet interesting people and feel that you are a part of the college community.

If you are a recent high school graduate 18-21 years of age, it is especially important for you to become involved in college activities. Perhaps you wish you could go away to school, but that shouldn't stop you from taking advantage of what a community college has to offer. Students your age can and do have a wonderful time during their community college years. They also receive out-of-class opportunities that are frequently unavailable to freshmen and sophomores in a university. Not having to compete with juniors and seniors does have its benefits.

The Fifth Benefit: New Friendships

Students in community colleges form deep and lasting friendships. If you ask a group of community college students ready to graduate what they liked about the experience, they will often tell you that they met people who became good friends. In this respect, community college students are similar to students in other colleges. A recent survey asked 2,379 graduating seniors from nine colleges what factors contributed significantly to a successful and satisfying college career. The most prevalent response by far was "personal contact with [other] students."

This news is hardly surprising. Friends are an important part of life, and we seek them wherever we go. But community college students have more than the usual reasons for forming new friendships. For them, friends are a source of mutual encouragement and support. Friends cheer each other on, ride to school together, baby-sit for each other and help one another through tough classes and tough times.

Frequently, our most satisfying friendships come from shared experiences. So it is with community college students. Open yourself to the possibility of new friends, and you may find a lasting, unexpected reward of your community college education.

The Sixth Benefit: Listening to People with Different Backgrounds and Points of View

Before long, you will encounter fellow students whose opinions and life experiences are quite different from your own. The process of discussing ideas with them is an especially valuable part of the collegiate experience. If you are like most community college students, you will enjoy the give and take of classroom dialogue and learn a great deal from it.

You will also be better prepared for the workplace of today and tomorrow. Employers are now looking for individuals who can work well in groups and teams. Many people possess the technical skills needed to perform their jobs, but not everyone has the ability to listen carefully, handle disagreements and work towards group solutions to problems. Your discussions with other students will help you participate in similar processes at work.

In addition, your classroom discussions will give you an opportunity to communicate with people of different cultures and nationalities. These encounters will fascinate you and open your eyes to new ways of looking at our society and the world. They will also help you develop empathy, the ability to understand and appreciate the perceptions and feelings of others. Empathy is important in all human relationships, but it is particularly essential when people do not share a common cultural background. As you continue to live and work in a culturally diverse society, you will find that your community college experience is of enormous benefit.

The Seventh Benefit: Becoming a More Self Aware, Resourceful and Fulfilled Human Being

A story, like a picture, is worth a thousand words. What follows are the personal accounts of four graduating community college students. Their names have been changed.

JACK, AGE 24

When I started on my associate degree, I was getting nowhere. I was working part-time in a drug store for minimum wage. I also had no real goal; I thought about being a corrections officer because they make a fortune in overtime. But the idea of working in a prison depressed me, so I gave that up.

One day another guy at the drug store suggested I take a business course. I took "Intro. to Business" and liked it. Then I took "Management" and liked that, too.

It even made the drug store more interesting. I began noticing things and came up with an idea for changing some of the displays. About six months after that, the manager offered me a full-time job with fringe benefits. He also said I might be eligible for their management training program.

Now, I'm about to graduate with an associate degree in Business Administration. I'm even thinking of transferring, although I'll probably take a break first. I don't know if I'll stay at the drug store, but I'm pretty set on a business career.

MARIE, AGE 37

It's hard to explain what college did for me. I know it has affected me in a lot of ways. I was the first one in my family to attend college, and I didn't know if I could do it. After all, I was a high school dropout who went back and got a G.E.D. I'm really proud of myself for staying with it.

It's funny, but one of the best things that happened is that I got the confidence to stick up for my daughter. She had problems in school, and I was always getting calls from the principal's office. I didn't always agree with her teachers or this assistant principal at the school. But, I was afraid to say anything. I'd just clam up. Talk about frustration! And my daughter was just getting worse and worse.

A year and a half ago, I was called in for another conference. It started out the same way, but suddenly I found myself talking. And once I started, I really got into it. For the first time, I told them how I really felt and what I thought should be done for my daughter. I stumbled a little bit, but I said what I wanted. Well, that was a turning point. My daughter still has some problems, but things are a lot better.

I can't tell you exactly what college has to do with this. I just know that it does. Before I came back to school, I was terrified of talking to those people. I guess I've changed.

JOHN, AGE 20

I really wasn't too happy about coming to a community college. I wanted to go away to school, but my dad lost his job. What made it a little better is that some of my friends from high school come here, too.

The part I hated most was living at home. Here I was in college and still arguing with the folks.

It also didn't seem like a real college. I thought a community college was just for people who couldn't get in somewhere else. Boy, was I wrong! The classes have been a lot tougher than I thought they would be. But they've been really interesting, too. Some of the students here are incredible. At first, I was spooked at being in classes with "older" people, but I got over that. Actually, the classes are a lot better that way. You can have a decent discussion. Some of my friends who go to universities are in really large classes where nobody's over 19. You don't get much out of that. A couple of them are here now because they just couldn't handle it.

I became involved with the school paper and really enjoyed that. I'll be transferring next year and feel ready for it. I'll still be living at home, but that's okay. Things have gotten better with the folks, and I'm not home that much, anyway. I think I've really grown up a lot the last couple of years.

GLORIA, AGE 44

I can't believe I'm about to graduate. It took me years to decide to come here because I was worried about my English. It's hard to think in English after thinking in Spanish for a long time.

I did it for my children. I'm always telling them they have to get an education, they have to go to college. Now, they have no excuse. If I did it, they can, too.

They're really proud of me, I know. The whole family will be at graduation. We'll celebrate!

What do these stories illustrate? For one thing, they demonstrate that people grow in self awareness during their community college years. Students have a chance to reflect on who they are, where their interests lie and what is truly important to them. Many people begin without a goal and develop one along the way. Many others arrive with a goal in mind but change it along the way. The community college journey is a time for self discovery.

It's also a time for becoming more resourceful. People grow in confidence and ability during their years in a community college. They are able and willing to attempt things they've never tried before. In the process, they become stronger human beings, capable of helping themselves and their loved ones.

Finally, the personal accounts of the four students illustrate a deep sense of personal accomplishment. When people complete their studies in a community college, they know they have

11

achieved something important and meaningful. For some, it's the fulfillment of a dream they never thought possible. For others, it's a milestone, the passage from one stage of life to another. For all, it's a time to celebrate and look back with satisfaction and pride.

The Benefits Begin Now

The best part of all is that the benefits of a community college education begin immediately. It's not just the degree or certificate at the end that matters; it's the process along the way. Each semester you enroll, you will acquire new skills, learn more about yourself and others and grow in ability and confidence. By choosing to attend a community college, you truly have made a wise decision.

NOW, LET'S TALK

After every chapter, you should talk about what you've read. You will get the most you can out of the book that way, and it will be more enjoyable to read.

Conversation 1: Talk with the Author

Obviously, you can't talk with the author if he isn't there. But imagine that he is. What would you say to him? What questions would you ask him? Did he say anything that was new or interesting to you? Did he say anything that you doubt or seems to contradict what you've heard before? Again, it's important to imagine that you're preparing to talk with a real person. You may want to go back and reread sections of the chapter. Feel free to write notes in the margin like, "not sure about this" or "never thought about that" or "don't understand what you mean by this." Write your comments and questions in the space below. Use additional paper if necessary. Be sure to put down any questions or thoughts that you have. Think hard.

_____

_____

_____

_____

_____

_____

_____

Conversation 2: Talk with the Teacher or Member of the College Staff

As you think about chapter one, what questions or thoughts do you have about your own community college? Again, think hard. When you talk to a teacher or member of the college staff, you want to be prepared, so that you can get as much as possible out of the conversation. Write your questions and comments here, but feel free to use additional paper. Go back and reread sections of the chapter if you want and write notes to yourself in the margin.

_____

_____

_____

_____

_____

_____

Conversation 3: Talk with Your Fellow Students

After reading chapter one, what would you like to know abut your fellow students? What would you like them to know about you? Write your thoughts and questions here. Use more paper if necessary.

_____

_____

_____

_____

Conversation 4: Talk with Friends and Family

After thinking about chapter one, what would you like to discuss with your friends or members of your family? Make notes to yourself below. Think about how you would begin the conversation.

_____

_____

_____

_____

_____

_____

_____

Conversation 5: Talk with Yourself

This is the most important conversation of all. What are you thinking about now? How are you feeling about beginning college? What steps do you need to take to get the most you can out of your community college experience?

_____

_____

_____

_____

_____

_____

_____

— Chapter 2 —

MAKING ACADEMIC DECISIONS

Chapter one mentioned that many community college students arrive without a specific academic goal, and even more change their academic goals before they finish. The process of making academic decisions occurs throughout a person's education, not just at the beginning

One of the difficulties facing new students is the bewildering variety of academic choices community colleges offer. How does a person select from so many possibilities? What are the advantages and disadvantages of each academic choice? What are the differences between academic programs that seem to have similar titles? Anyone would be confused.

This chapter will not list the academic choices at your community college. You will need to ask about the options available to you or find a listing of academic programs in the college catalog.

What this chapter will do is explain the types of academic programs offered by community colleges and what each type is designed to accomplish. After reading the chapter, it will be much easier for you to make sense of the choices available at your school.

You probably know by now that community colleges award associate degrees. However, you may not know that they offer non-degree opportunities as well. To explore the options available to you, you need to understand both possibilities.

17

The Associate Degree Path

Almost all community colleges award two kinds of associate degrees, the Associate in Arts degree, commonly called the A.A., and the Associate in Science degree, commonly called the A.S. Some community colleges also award the Associate in Applied Science degree, commonly referred to as the A.A.S.

The academic programs leading to each of these degrees have different purposes and requirements. But they also have much in common. The next section explains the common features of the various degree programs, and the section following explains their differences.

What Associate Degree Programs Have in Common

Associate degree programs have three characteristics in common:

A Program of Study. Sometimes called a "curriculum," a program of study is a well planned series of courses leading to the associate degree. The program of study includes courses students must take, sometimes labelled "core" or "required" courses as well as "elective" courses that students may choose themselves. Some programs of study are more prescriptive than others; that is they include more core or required courses and fewer electives. The reasons for this difference will be discussed later.

A program of study also includes the sequence or order in which courses must be taken. A word you will see or hear is "prerequisite." If a course has a prerequisite, it means that another course must be completed before that one. Similarly, if a course has a "co-requisite," it means that another course must be taken at the same time.

Each community college has its own way of displaying programs of study. Usually, the catalog contains all of the programs of study offered by a college, but you should ask to make sure.

18

A Minimum Number of Credits. An associate degree requires the completion of a minimum of 60 semester credits. Some programs of study require the completion of more than 60 semester credits, but all require at least 60. If your college offers classes in quarters or trimesters, the number of credits required for graduation will be different, although equivalent to 60 semester credits.

The number of semester credits you receive for completing a course depends on the number of hours you spend in class. The general rule is that you receive one credit for every fifteen hours that a class meets. Thus, if a class meets for 45 hours during a semester, you will receive three credits for completing it. There are exceptions to this rule, especially for courses with a lab, but it holds true in most cases.

Classes can be offered for any number of credits, but the typical class is offered for three credits. During a fifteen week semester, a three credit class usually meets for three hours per week. During a shorter semester, such as a summer term, the number of classroom hours per week will be greater.

If students take only three credit classes, they will need to complete twenty classes in order to earn 60 credits. Remember that 60 semester credits is a minimum number for the associate degree, and that some programs of study require more.

This explanation is based on semester credits because most community colleges calculate credits that way. If your community college does not, a member of the college staff can explain the difference to you.

General Education Requirements. Any program of study leading to an associate degree requires a number of courses devoted to a student's general education. Courses in this category emphasize the knowledge and abilities needed by all adults in our society, regardless of their separate interests or careers.

Many general education courses come from the academic areas known as the liberal arts. These areas include:

- **The Humanities**. Often called the study of truth, beauty and goodness, the Humanities encompass a wide range of academic fields or "disciplines." Among them are: English; Philosophy; Religion; Communication; Foreign Languages; Art; Music; Drama; and other visual or performing arts.

- **The Social Sciences.** Courses in the Social Sciences focus on how people behave individually and in groups or societies. Among the disciplines represented are: Anthropology; Psychology; Sociology; Economics; History; Political Science; and Geography.

- **The Natural Sciences.** The Natural Sciences include the Physical and Biological Sciences. Among its disciplines are: Astronomy; Chemistry; Physics; Geology; Biology; and Environmental Science.

- **Mathematics.** Some community colleges link Math with Natural Science, but most have separate Math requirements. The courses offered vary from college to college but usually include: general courses in Math theory; support courses for other disciplines, such as Business Math; and several levels of Algebra, Statistics, Calculus and Differential Equations.

The titles of some liberal arts courses correspond to the disciplines from which they come, like "Introduction to Psychology." But others have titles like "The Individual in a Changing Society" or "The Politics of the Environment." Courses in this latter category may be interdisciplinary, which means that they include knowledge from more than one discipline.

Besides liberal arts courses, community colleges can have other general education requirements. For example, some colleges require all of their students to take a course in Basic Microcomputer Applications, while others require a course in Health Maintenance or Fitness.

New students often ask why they must take general education courses, especially if these courses do not seem connected to their interests or career goals. The central reason is that a college education challenges us to expand our interests and examine our goals. As Charles M. Vest, President of the Massachusetts Institute of Technology put it, a college education "is to provide the means for us to understand ourselves and the contemporary and historical currents that affect what we believe and the choices we make."

Think back for a moment to chapter one. A number of the benefits of a community college education were economic or career related, but several were not. They had more to do with the benefits to us as people; our awareness of self, our relationships with others and our capacity to act on behalf of ourselves and our loved ones. Kathryn Moorman, President of Colorado College, raised an important point when she noted that "on average, Americans spend 90,000 hours over a lifetime on the job, but five times that number - 450,000 hours - as neighbors, parents, spouses, and voters." General education encourages us to look at every part of our adult lives. Nothing could be more valuable than that.

But the value of general education doesn't stop there. It also helps us to fulfill our career goals. To see why, ask yourself this question: Do you really know what knowledge and skills will be useful to you on the job? To some extent, you probably do, but what if you are faced with a strange or unexpected situation? For example, what if you wind up in the middle of a heated argument among co-workers, and everyone wants you to take sides? What if a co-worker has a problem with alcohol or drug abuse, and it is beginning to affect your work as well? What if you have been asked to take a lie detector test because "someone" has been stealing from the employer? What if your boss wants you to work on something in a group, but one of your co-workers insists that he already has all the answers? In these situations, you will be thankful for a strong general education.

Now ask yourself three additional questions:

✓ Do you really know what knowledge and abilities you will need in the future?
✓ Can you predict what job you will have five or ten years from now?
✓ Do you know how many times you will need retraining during that period?

If you are honest, the answer to all three questions is likely to be no. In a rapidly changing economy, few people can predict how their careers will unfold. Knowledge that seemed irrelevant yesterday may suddenly become critical today. Your best bet is to develop a variety of skills, a storehouse of knowledge and an appetite for further learning. In short, an excellent career education includes an excellent general education.

So now you are familiar with the common ingredients of all associate degree programs: a planned program of study; a minimum credit requirement; and a strong foundation in general education. The next section explains how associate degree programs differ from each other.

Different Degree Programs for Different Purposes

As noted before, almost all community colleges award two types of associate degrees, the Associate in Arts (A.A.) and the Associate in Science (A.S.), and some schools award a third type, the Associate in Applied Science (A.A.S.). Unfortunately, it is difficult to generalize about the purpose of each of these degrees. At some colleges, only one type of degree program, the A.A., is intended for the student who wishes to transfer to a university, but at other colleges, an A.S. degree program may fulfill that purpose, too. A member of the faculty or staff at your school will need to explain which degrees are awarded by your college and what purpose each one serves.

No matter how your school arranges its degrees, every program of study is designed to achieve one of three purposes:

To prepare a student for transfer to a university. The transfer degree program ensures that a student is well prepared for the junior year in a university. Required courses in the program of study are determined in consultation with area or state universities. The result is an "articulation agreement" which guarantees that courses taken at the community college will be accepted by the university. An academic adviser at your college can explain how this process works in your region.

Transfer degree programs usually require additional liberal arts courses beyond the basic general education requirements. The emphasis on liberal arts courses is to ensure that a student has a well rounded education and all of the academic abilities needed for success in the junior year.

For a similar reason, transfer degree programs include a series of advanced course requirements, often at the 200 (Sophomore) level. These courses are more difficult, build on lower level courses and develop a strong academic foundation.

A word of caution. Community college students sometimes choose to transfer to a university before they have completed the associate degree. In individual cases, this may be a good decision, but it should be considered carefully. In some regions, articulation agreements between community colleges and universities only apply to those students who finish the associate degree. Furthermore, studies of community college students who transfer to a university show that they tend to do better if they have completed the associate degree first. Again, the decision to transfer prematurely may be justified in an individual case, but a student should always see an academic adviser before making the change.

To prepare the student for a career. The career degree program, sometimes called the occupational degree program, is designed to prepare a student for work upon graduation. Almost

23

always, career degree programs lead to the Associate in Science (A.S.) or Associate in Applied Science (A.A.S.) degrees.

Like all associate degree programs, the career program includes a number of required general education courses, but its main focus is preparation for a particular occupation. To make sure that the program fulfills that purpose, faculty members meet regularly with an advisory council of employers and practitioners in the field.

Career programs blend theory and practice. Students read, listen to lectures and discuss how the information they've learned can be applied to various work situations. At different points in the program, they also have an opportunity to meet individuals employed in the field and to gain hands-on experience as interns or practicum students.

Many people who complete career programs eventually decide to go on for further education. As a new student, you should be open to this possibility. The associate degree is an important step up the educational and professional ladder but often not the last.

To provide an opportunity for general study. Some community colleges offer a third type of degree program that is less prescriptive than the other two. Sometimes called General Studies, this degree program allows students to choose more electives and to build a flexible program of study.

The General Studies program is designed for students who have not decided on an area of interest or have special interests that cannot be met within the requirements of other degrees. With the assistance of an academic adviser, a student can create a program of study that is suitable for transfer to a university, preparation for a career or a combination of both. Occasionally, General Studies students simply want to pursue a college education for intellectual stimulation and personal growth.

Please remember that not every community college offers this type of degree. If your school offers it, and you are interested, be sure to talk to an academic adviser. The General Studies program is right for some people but not for everyone.

You now have an overview of the associate degree and the different types of degree programs that are available to you. The next section discusses the non-degree options offered by most community colleges.

The Non-Degree Path

Almost all community colleges award certificates as well as associate degrees. Programs of study leading to a certificate usually include 24-36 semester credits, roughly half the number required for a degree. Certificate programs may be in completely different areas than degree programs, or they may be in the same areas. For example, a college might offer an associate degree program and a certificate program in Accounting. The certificate program would include some of the same courses but fewer total credits.

Students sometimes enroll in certificate programs as a stepping stone to the associate degree. With the certificate, they are able to improve their short-term job prospects and make the rest of their education easier. Occasionally, people enroll in a degree program in one area and a certificate program in another. There are numerous possibilities.

A smaller percentage of students take courses without enrolling in any degree or certificate program. They may want to acquire new skills, like computer skills, or simply take classes of personal interest. Some already have associate or even higher degrees but feel the need for continuing education.

Now What?

Now you are ready to look at the options offered by your college. Usually, the college catalog includes a description of all degrees and certificate programs, and academic advisers are available to assist. Just remember two principles that will be repeated over and over again in this book. This first is that you can change your mind. As people learn more about themselves and the options available to them, they often change their academic programs. The second principle is that you can get help, but you have to ask. Community colleges have faculty and staff to guide you, but you have to take the initiative. If you're not sure who to ask, approach any member of the faculty or staff. With a bit of patience, you'll find the individual you need.

NOW, LETS TALK

Chapter two contained a great deal of information. To apply the information, you need to ask questions and discuss your thoughts with others.

Conversation 1: Talk with the Author

As before, imagine that you will have a conversation with the author. What questions do you have? Did he say anything that made you think differently about the choices available to you? If necessary, review sections of the chapter and make notes in the margin. Write your comments and questions below. Use additional paper as needed.

_____

_____

_____

_____

_____

_____

_____

_____

_____

_____

Conversation 2: Talk with the Teacher or Member of the College Staff

What questions or thoughts do you now have about the academic programs at your own community college? Think hard. This is an important one.

_____

_____

_____

_____

_____

_____

_____

Conversation 3: Talk with your Fellow Students

Don't limit yourself to new students like yourself. After reading chapter two, what would you like to discuss with students who have attended your college for a while? How about students enrolled in particular degree or certificate programs? Can you think of questions you would like to ask people who recently graduated from your college?

_____

_____

_____

_____

_____

_____

Conversation 4: Talk with Friends and Family

As a result of reading chapter two, what would you like to discuss with your friends or family? Make notes to yourself below. Think about how you would begin the conversation.

_____

_____

_____

_____

_____

_____

_____

Conversation 5: Talk with Yourself

Again, this is the most important conversation of all. What are your thoughts now? Do you need additional information? If so, how do you plan to get it?

_____

_____

_____

_____

_____

_____

_____

_____

Chapter 3

WHAT IT TAKES TO DO WELL

This chapter begins with a personal introduction. My name is Wayne Silver, and I am the author of the book you are reading. I am also a faculty member at Three Rivers Community-Technical College, a school with 4,000 students in Norwich, Connecticut. Before coming to Connecticut, I was a faculty member at Miami-Dade Community College, a school with 60,000 students in Miami, Florida. During my careers in both places, I served as an academic administrator and had the opportunity to observe dozens of classes and hundreds of students.

I am going to speak to you openly and directly. At points, I'll plead with you or even try to scare you a little. My goal is to get your community college education off on the right foot. I hope you will listen and consider my ideas carefully.

Two Realities

Let me begin with two facts of life. The first is that not everyone does well in community college classes. Students who arrive with strong academic backgrounds have an advantage, but even they sometimes experience difficulty. College is quite different from high school, and it requires a significant adjustment.

The second fact is critical: Almost everyone can do well in a community college. I don't mean that all students are capable of getting A's or B's in every course. That simply isn't real life. But nearly all have the ability to earn an associate degree or certificate, even if they arrive with weak academic backgrounds and many years of prior school frustration.

A community college education is a new beginning. It provides an opportunity for people to become successful students, but it doesn't guarantee it.

The Ingredients of Doing Well

There are several ways to find out how students do well in their classes. You can interview "good" students and ask them how they do it. You can ask teachers to explain what they expect from students. Or you can catch students in the act of doing well and observe their behavior.

I've done all three and want to share the results with you. Some of the principles of doing well will seem obvious, but they're not. In each case, there are reasons why people are unaware of them, misunderstand them or even resist them. As you read, please keep an open mind and follow my explanations to the end.

The First Principle: Come to Class

Surely, this is the most obvious principle of all. You're probably saying to yourself that it's not even worth discussing. Of course you have to attend classes regularly in order to do well.

But it isn't so obvious once you start. Many community college instructors do not have formal attendance requirements. They may "suggest" that students attend regularly, but that it is a matter of individual choice. A few may not even mention attendance at all.

As a new student, you can become confused by these mixed signals. You could easily interpret an instructor's comments (or lack of comments) to mean that attendance isn't so important after all. Maybe you can get away with skipping classes here and there as long as you read the book and "check in" once in a while.

What a mistake! Regular attendance is essential, even when the teacher fails to make a point of it. The reasons some teachers do not require attendance are: they assume you already know how important attendance is and will act accordingly; they respect you as an adult learner and do not want to "force" you to attend class; they believe that you should learn the importance of attendance the hard way, by failing a test or even a course; or they simply don't want to be bothered with the task of taking attendance.

But they never mean that regular attendance is unimportant. Numerous studies demonstrate the relationship between attendance and classroom success. No matter how hard students try on their own, most cannot succeed without frequent interaction with their teachers and classmates.

So don't be misled. Plan to attend class, **every** class. Emergencies arise, but they are few and far between. Remember that your academic success rests on coming to class.

The Second Principle: Do the Work

Like the first principle, this one is trickier that it first appears. College courses require **substantial** work outside of class. An often used formula is that students must spend two hours outside of class for every hour in it. This figure varies from course to course and individual to individual, but it emphasizes the need for concentrated study outside of class.

New students are sometimes shocked by the amount of work assigned by their teachers. Unfortunately, their prior school experiences included little if any work that could not be completed in class itself. By the same token, their previous teachers were not especially concerned about deadlines. As one student said to me, "my high school teachers were grateful if we handed in anything; if they got something on time, they nearly passed out." College teachers not only expect students to complete their assignments; they expect the work to be handed in when it is due.

At times, new students intend to do the work but haven't built enough hours for study into their weekly schedules. This is understandable when people are unaware of what to expect or when they are trying to juggle school, a job and home responsibilities. Chapter five discusses the delicate balancing act many students carry out and gives practical advice on how to manage it.

As schoolwork piles up, it is tempting to retreat from it. Professor John Langan of Atlantic Community College notes that students engage in "avoidance tactics" to keep from doing assigned work. Among the excuses they offer themselves are:

> "I can't do it."
> "I'm too busy."
> "I'm too tired."
> "I'll do it later."
> "I'm bored with the subject."

You need to guard against these self defeating excuses. Professor Langan sums it up this way:

> *Your attitude must say, "I will do the work." I have found that among the two hundred or so students I meet each year, there is almost no way of telling at first which ones have this attitude and which ones do not. Some time must pass for people to reveal their attitude by what they do or do not do. What happens is that as the semester unfolds and classes must be attended and work must be done, some people take on the work and persist even if they hit all kinds of snags and problems; others don't take on the work or don't persist when things get rough. It becomes clear which students have determined inside themselves, "I will do the work," and which have not.*

Professor Langan is right. Determination matters. Resolve now that you will do the work, no matter what. It will be the most important decision you make during your community college journey.

The Third Principle: Do the Work Well

While it's essential to do the work, it's still not enough. You must do the work **well.** Your teachers are concerned with the quality of your work and will grade you accordingly.

This, too, can be a shock. I've met many new students who were honestly confused after being told that a piece of work was unacceptable. Their former teachers had required only that they complete assignments, not that they complete assignments well. The emphasis was on the quantity of the work, not its quality.

College instructors insist on quality as well as quantity. Grading is fair but rigorous and demanding. Consider it a compliment. Your teachers expect a great deal from you because they regard you as a serious and capable learner.

Remember that help is available when you need it. Community colleges offer many forms of academic assistance, including tutoring, study groups and preparatory classes. Each of these will be explained later, but the key point is that you're not alone. Your college wants you to do well and will support you in that effort.

The Fourth Principle: Do the Work Well Even if the Teacher's Not So Great

I'm going to start this section by going out on a limb. My prediction is that you will be pleased with most of your teachers. Community colleges pride themselves on the excellence of their teachers and choose them carefully.

But you probably won't be pleased with all of them. Teachers differ widely in how they conduct their classes, and you will prefer some to others. You may also find that it is easier to learn in some classes than others. Perhaps the instructors explain things more clearly or give helpful hints on how to study the material.

But whether you like the teacher or not, you are responsible for completing high quality work. Al Siebert and Timothy Walter, co-authors of *Student Success*, believe that one of the main reasons students experience frustration in college is that they "can't handle the change from a teaching environment to a learning environment." During their previous school years, much of their learning depended on the teacher; now the responsibility rests with them. It's a major transition.

So begin now to change your thinking about teaching and learning. The goal is to learn well in every course, not to be taught well in every course. An excellent teacher is a pleasant bonus but not something you can expect all the time.

The Fifth Principle: Study and Participate Enthusiastically

This principle is especially important. Successful students approach their classes enthusiastically. They "get into" the whole process of reading, completing assignments, listening to lectures and joining in classroom activities or discussions.

To study and participate enthusiastically, you first have to get away from the idea that education is something "done to you." Many of us are raised with this notion. We believe that we receive education from a teacher, like we receive pills from a doctor. If we show up and open our empty heads, the teacher will pour in the information we need.

The truth is that we learn little this way. It is difficult to remember and use information we haven't thought about, discussed or tried to apply to our lives. That's why at the end of chapters one and two, you were asked to talk about what you had read. I wanted you to imagine that you could have a real conversation with me, ask me questions, agree or disagree. Then, I wanted

36

you to share your ideas with others and listen carefully to theirs. Finally, I wanted you to mull things over and arrive at conclusions that made sense to you. During the process, I encouraged you to reread sections of the chapters, scribble in the margins and write about your reactions. In short, I asked you to be an enthusiastic learner.

Not every course will offer the same kinds of opportunities for enthusiastic learning. A math class is different from a history class. But every course can be approached enthusiastically in some way. It simply requires asking questions, thinking about what you are doing and participating actively in class.

Perhaps this type of involvement in your learning is new to you. If so, you may need to take a risk in order to try it. Remember that you don't need to accomplish everything at once. You just need to get a start. Write in the book. Ask a question. State an opinion or reaction. Ask somebody else for an opinion or reaction. Volunteer for an activity in class. Get started.

The Sixth Principle: Get Help When You Need It (Or Even Before)

If you experience difficulty in a class, don't wait. Seek help immediately. The first step, of course, is to talk to the instructor. Usually, full-time faculty have regular office hours set aside for this purpose. Part-time faculty may not have scheduled hours, but they are available by appointment.

New students are often reluctant to talk to their teachers outside of class. They fear that they will "look stupid" or that they will "bother the teacher." At times, they're just not sure how to state the source of their difficulty.

Let's deal with these fears now. It is an important part of a community college teacher's job to help students outside of class. You're not bothering the instructor by asking for assistance. In fact, she or he will be grateful. What teachers fear most is that they will discover a student's distress after it is too late to do anything about it. The student who comes forward before there is a crisis makes the teacher's job easier, not harder.

If you're not sure why you're experiencing difficulty in a class, don't worry about it. Teachers are used to that. They can help you figure out the reason for your frustration and advise you on how to overcome it.

You should also talk to the teacher if you must be absent. You may be able to get an assignment in advance or arrange to get missing class notes. If you cannot notify the teacher in advance, you should communicate with him or her as soon as possible. A personal conference is best, but a phone call is a good alternative.

Occasionally, a student will have more than the usual discomfort about seeing a teacher outside of class. Perhaps a teacher isn't very approachable, or the student is especially shy. If you find yourself in this situation, it's important to talk to someone else. Community colleges have counselors who can offer good advice. The worst thing you can do is to keep your problems to yourself.

Remember, too, that community colleges generally offer individual or small group tutoring for students who need it. Talking to the teacher is the first step but not the only step. Help is available, but you must take the initiative to ask for it.

The Seventh Principle: Help Your Classmates and Let Them Help You

Recall chapter one for a moment. One of the benefits of a community college education was the formation of lasting friendships. Another was the opportunity to discuss ideas with people different from yourself. Both of these benefits emphasize the importance of student-to-student relationships in a community college education.

But of more immediate concern, the relationships you establish with your classmates will help you (and them) become better students. Students enrolled in the same classes assist each other in many ways, including:

- **Studying together.** It is often helpful to study with another person who is reading or reviewing the same material. Study partners can quiz each other, go over difficult concepts together or simply encourage each other to keep going. A more elaborate arrangement is the study group involving several classmates. Usually, study groups meet before class sessions to review assigned reading, go over lecture notes and prepare for exams. Some community colleges provide assistance to students who want to form study groups, but you'll have to ask about that.

- **Calling each other for help.** At times, schedule conflicts prevent people from studying with others. However, trading phone numbers with one or more classmates can be a valuable alternative. You can agree to call each other with questions or problems. Often, phone partners agree to share class notes in the event that any of them must be absent.

- **Brainstorming together.** When you receive a challenging assignment, it is useful to discuss it with other students. By talking about it, the two (or more) of you will have a better understanding of the assignment and the possible ways to approach it. It's also a great way to come up with ideas. Two (or three or four) heads are better than one.

- **Giving feedback to each other.** Successful students often look at each other's work before handing it in. They may offer suggestions for improvement or simply spot minor errors that need to be corrected. Sometimes, the best teacher is another student.

- **Approaching an instructor together.** The last section discussed why new students may be reluctant to see an instructor. If you need to talk to your teacher but feel hesitant, take a classmate with you. You'll feel more comfortable, and your classmate will probably benefit too.

39

All of these ways that classmates help each other require some-one to take the initiative. Someone must offer to trade phone numbers or form a study partnership. Why not be the one to get the ball rolling? You'll be helping yourself and someone else.

The Eighth Principle: Move Slowly When You Must

There are times when community college students just can't progress as quickly as they would like. For some, the reason is that they must spend time at the beginning improving their abilities in reading, writing or math. If you are in this category, you are not alone. It is quite common for new community college students to need preparatory (sometimes called developmental or basic) courses before they are ready for more difficult classes. Perhaps they have been out of school for a while, or they simply did not get a strong background in particular areas.

People who take preparatory classes are making a wise invest-ment of time and effort. These classes work! Students who ap-proach them seriously have a good chance of succeeding in their later courses. By the same token. students who take classes to build their study skills heighten their performance in all of their courses. It is worth the additional time at the beginning to im-prove the chances of academic success later.

Another reason that many community college students need to move slowly is that they have other responsibilities and can only attend school part-time. Chapter five discusses this common situation and how people deal with it. For now, just remember that thousands of community college students work, raise fami-lies and complete associate degrees or certificates. Patience pays off. Remember, too, that the benefits of a community college edu-cation occur immediately and at every step along the way. The process may take a while, but it's worth it.

The Ninth Principle: If Necessary, Shed the Past

None of us can shed the past completely. We all bring our past experiences into our present thoughts and activities. But this doesn't mean that we are prisoners of the past. We can and do move beyond our past experiences when they interfere with our goals and dreams.

Sometimes, new community college students need to do that. Perhaps their past experiences taught them that they are " bad students " or that they " can't do it " or that school is painful and frustrating. These old beliefs have a way of surfacing time and again.

But the past can be put in its proper place. It's not easy, and it doesn't happen over- night. People learn gradually through their day-to-day community college experiences that they are capable students, and that they belong in college.

The community college journey marks a new beginning. It's an opportunity not only to become a successful student but to see yourself as one. Roll with it for a while. You may be surprised.

The Tenth Principle: Develop a Life as a College Student

Elaine Pelliccio, a faculty colleague of mine at Three Rivers Community-Technical College, recently made the following observation:

> *Students need to develop a student life. They develop lives as parents, lives as employees, but somehow neglect to develop a life for the student. By this I mean, they devote just enough time to come to class and to return home to do homework, and that's it. College is not simply an add-on to their old routine. They need to understand the importance of becoming involved in college*

41

affairs or attending college functions. The sense of "con-
nectedness" to the college might actually help them
through academic turbulence even more than an extra
study hour or two at home.

Ms. Pelliccio's point is a critical one. A community college is a small (or not so small) community of its own, and it is important to feel that you are a part of it. Even if your schedule is busy, you can read your college newspaper and attend a college event once in a while. You will enjoy it, meet interesting people and experience the sense of involvement and belonging that is often necessary for academic success.

Conclusion

I want to restate a point raised earlier: Community colleges provide an opportunity for people to become successful students, but there are no guarantees. Students must decide that they want to be successful and begin to take the steps necessary to achieve that goal. The ten principles outlined in this chapter provide an excellent starting point. The next chapter explains the resources available to students as they make the adjustment to college life.

NOW LETS TALK

You now know how important it is to think and talk about what you've read. It's part of becoming an enthusiastic learner.

Conversation 1: Talk with the Author

You still have to imagine but not quite as much. You know at least a few things about me. Did I say anything in chapter three that made you think differently? Was there anything you doubted? As before, review sections of the chapter and make notes in the margin. Write your comments and questions below. Use additional paper as needed.

_____

_____

_____

_____

_____

_____

_____

_____

_____

_____

_____

Conversation 2: Talk with the Teacher or Member of the College Staff

What questions do you now have about classes, teachers or other students at your own college? Think hard. This is an important one.

_____

_____

_____

_____

_____

_____

_____

Conversation 3: Talk with your Fellow Students

Remember how important it is to help other students and let them help you. After reading chapter three, what would you like to discuss with one or more of your classmates?

_____

_____

_____

_____

_____

_____

_____

Conversation 4: Talk with Friends and Family

Do you think any of the information in chapter three would be a surprise to friends or family members? Is there anything you would like to discuss with them now? Make notes to yourself below. Think about how you would begin the conversation.

_____

_____

_____

_____

_____

_____

_____

Conversation 5: Talk with Yourself

As always, this is the most important conversation of all. What are your thoughts now? What steps can you take to apply the ten principles in chapter three to your own life?

_____

_____

_____

_____

_____

_____

_____

— Chapter 4 —

SEEKING HELP

Community college students need help for a variety of reasons. Some have difficulty in their classes and require individual or small group assistance. Others need help in making academic or career decisions. Still more need assistance in completing all of the forms and "bureaucratic" tasks that community colleges require. And many need help in removing or working around stumbling blocks that interfere with their ability to stay in college. These obstacles differ from person to person but often include: lack of money to pay school and living expenses; unreliable transportation; unpredictable work schedules; inadequate child care; and family troubles or emergencies.

Again, I am going to speak to you frankly and openly. At times, the difficulties experienced by community college students are not easily overcome. For new students especially, they can appear overwhelming. It takes a while to work out solutions to complex problems.

But help is available. Community colleges provide many forms of assistance to their students. Furthermore, as students start to meet, they find ways of helping each other. The last chapter discussed how students enrolled in the same classes assist one another, but that's only the beginning. Students help each others in ways you've never imagined.

Sadly, some community college students decide to discontinue their education without ever asking for help. They either don't know where or how to seek assistance, or they assume that help is unavailable for their particular problem. Occasionally, they are embarrassed or believe that asking for help is a sign of personal weakness.

Please don't make that mistake. Seek help as soon as you need it. I'm not saying every problem can be fixed. Life doesn't always cooperate. But many problems facing community college students can be resolved or, at least, reduced.

The next section explains how community colleges assist their students directly or through referral to community resources. The section following looks at student-to-student relationships and the creative ways that students work together for mutual benefit.

How Community Colleges Help

Occasionally, community college faculty and staff are able to provide an immediate answer to a problem. But more often than not, they give information, help identify options and explain the steps that are necessary to carry out a plan of action. The major responsibility for addressing the problem still rests with the student. College staff cannot remove that responsibility, nor should they. If people learn to resolve difficult issues during their community college years, they will be prepared for similar situations throughout their lives.

All community colleges do not offer the same services to students, nor do they have the same names or labels for the services they provide. However, nearly all offer the following:

Tutoring centers and learning labs. As I mentioned in the last chapter, almost all community colleges provide individual or small group tutoring. Some colleges do so in an "all purpose" tutoring center, while others have separate centers or labs for particular areas, such as writing, math, foreign languages, microcomputers or accounting. In addition to tutoring, many of these centers or labs sponsor workshops on important topics, help students to complete assignments or practice the skills they've learned in class and provide opportunities for individual, self-di-

48

rected learning. For example, a writing or computer lab might allow students to learn the basics of word processing and then practice on their own.

You should take a walking tour of all of the tutoring centers and learning labs at your college. They are valuable resources, and if you become familiar with them now, you are more likely to use them later.

Academic advisement. Community colleges differ in how they advise students. At some schools, faculty do all or most of the advising, while, at others, full-time academic advisers assume the primary role. The purposes of academic advisement are to help you select a program of study, ensure that you understand all of the requirements for program completion and to assist you in choosing courses for an upcoming semester. Advisers never make decisions for you, but they do make sure that you have all of the information needed to make decisions for yourself.

You can see your academic adviser as often as necessary. Students who are confused or undecided about what program of study is right for them may need additional sessions with an adviser. Remember, too, that many students change their programs of study (perhaps more than once) before they graduate. The academic adviser is a valuable resource at every stage of a person's community college education.

Career planning and placement. Like an academic adviser, a career planning counselor assists people in recognizing and evaluating the choices that are open to them. Students can receive information about a wide variety of careers and how they can match their personal interests and strengths with different options. Career counselors also provide assistance in locating jobs, preparing resumes and planning for interviews. For students who are working while they are in school, the career planning office maintains a list of local job opportunities.

Financial aid. The financial aid office provides information on grants, loans, work-study jobs and other forms of financial assistance. Even if you don't think you're eligible, it's worth a visit to the financial aid office to be sure.

Counseling. Counselors are available for short-term personal counseling. Conversations are private and confidential. Counselors help with learning related problems, such as difficulties in the classroom or with instructors, stress and test anxiety and balancing family, college and work. When necessary, they refer students to support groups or resources and agencies within the community.

Disabled student services. All community colleges have an office or staff member responsible for coordinating services to students with a disability. The disability can be long-standing or a temporary disability like a broken leg.

Not all disabilities are visible. For example, a learning disability can't be seen, but it is a disability just the same. Sometimes, people with this type of disability are unaware of it. They have struggled for years in school situations without ever understanding the reason. If you think you may have a learning or other disability but are not sure, make an appointment to see the disabled student counselor at your college.

Occasionally, students with a disability choose not to reveal that fact to the colleges they attend. They may fear that they will be "singled out," or that it will look like they are "asking for special favors." Perhaps they are embarrassed or feel that revealing a disability can lead to discrimination or some other harmful result.

Since I have a severe hearing loss, I can understand and appreciate these feelings. However, students with a disability usually benefit if they let the college know. By law and by choice, community colleges provide information, services and classroom accommodations.

If you have a disability but are reluctant to reveal it, you owe it to yourself to discuss this issue with the disabled student services coordinator. All conversations will be held in confidence, and any decision you reach will be respected.

Services for other categories of students. Community colleges vary considerably in how they organize their services. But almost all have a staff member with responsibility for meeting the needs of international students, and many have special programs or services for minority students, women and senior citizens. Some also have honors programs or chapters of Phi Theta Kappa, a national community college academic honor society.

College library. Use of the library is not only a central part of your education; it's also a resource for dealing with the problems of life. A community college library contains guides to community agencies and reference material on every subject imaginable. During the past year, students in my classes have used library information to set up a family budget, improve child-parent relationships, establish a small business in the home and confront a spouse with an alcohol abuse problem.

As soon as you can, you should take a walking tour of your college library. Don't be hesitant to ask questions or seek assistance from the librarians.

Day care. Not every community college offers day care for the children of its students, but many do. Some even have "Parent Centers" or other programs to assist students who are combining college with parenthood.

Student activities. Chapter one explained the wealth of community college opportunities beyond the classroom. The Office of Student Activities maintains a list of these opportunities and helps students who wish to start new groups or activities.

All faculty and staff. Every member of the faculty and staff is a potential source of help. Talk to anyone with whom you feel comfortable. The important thing is to seek assistance, even if that just means a friendly listener. Do not keep your problems to yourself. That's the worst mistake you can make.

How Students Help Each Other

The last chapter explained the ways that students enrolled in the same classes work together for mutual benefit. But community college students cooperate in many other ways as well. Let me give you a few examples:

Tutoring agreements. Students often agree to tutor each other. Perhaps one is stronger in English, and the other is stronger in math.

Transportation agreements. This is a common form of cooperation. Riding to class together has the additional benefit of allowing people to talk about their classes and school experiences.

Child care agreements. Students with children often babysit for each other. Some limit "child sharing" to class times, while others extend it to study periods as well.

Emergency agreements. Community college students frequently agree to help each other in the event of an emergency. Emergency assistance can take many forms, including transportation, alerting instructors or securing class notes.

Living agreements. This is the most elaborate agreement of all. Students sometimes choose to share a household in order to reduce expenses and pool their resources. I've known a number of single parents who found this type of arrangement to be of great benefit.

These student-to-student agreements are only a starting point. As you meet other students, you will think of additional ways that you can cooperate. Perhaps your school has a "ride-share" directory, bulletin boards (electronic or otherwise) or other channels to make communication easier. In any event, you must be open to the possibility of working with fellow students and look for opportunities to make it happen.

Conclusion

Seeking help can be a matter of academic survival, just like studying for a test. View it as a creative challenge and an important part of your education. Who knows? The problem solving abilities you acquire and the relationships you form with other students may turn out to be the most lasting benefits of the entire process.

NOW, LET'S TALK

This section asks you to think further about possible helping relationships.

Conversation 1: Talk with the Teacher or Member of the College Staff

By now, you must have many thoughts or questions about the resources available at your college. Which of these resources will be most helpful to you? Why?

_____

_____

_____

_____

_____

_____

_____

_____

_____

_____

_____

_____

_____

_____

Conversation 2: Talk with Your Fellow Students

As a result of reading chapter four, what would you like to know about other students at your college? Do you think you can co-operate with another student (or more) for mutual benefit? How?

_____

_____

_____

_____

_____

_____

_____

_____

Conversation 3: Talk with Yourself

Be honest. Are you likely to seek help when you need it? Why or why not? What help do you need now?

_____

_____

_____

_____

_____

_____

_____

_____

Chapter 5

DIFFERENT PEOPLE: DIFFERENT EXPERIENCES

One of the benefits of a community college education is the opportunity to meet and discuss ideas with people different from yourself. A typical classroom brings together men and women of different ages, races, political affiliations, life experiences and values. The dialogue among them exposes the rich variety in the human family as well as the feelings and aspirations that are common to us all.

Because community college students are so varied, they experience the educational process differently. The same is true of any human encounter. Three people can see a movie and experience it in completely different ways. One may be bored, one excited and one moved to tears.

In this chapter, I want to discuss the experiences of three types of community college students: the traditional age college student; the student balancing school, work or family responsibilities; and the student who is the first (or nearly the first) member of his or her family to attend college. I could have chosen many other kinds of students to discuss, but these three often have experiences that are difficult to anticipate. Naturally, it is possible, even common, for a person to belong to more than one of the three categories.

The Traditional Age College Student

The younger community college student, 18-21 years of age, faces some unusual challenges. The following narratives come from conversations with traditional age students who have attended a community college for two semesters or more. The names have been changed.

GEORGE

Well, I'm on my own, sort of. I moved out of the house at the end of last semester and now share an apartment with a friend of mine. It's tight, but with my job, I'm making it. My mom slips me a few bucks when my dad's not looking.

But, even though I'm on my own, I'm still in town. The [family] house is only a couple of miles away from my apartment. So my mom still wants me to stop by. Actually, it's not too bad. I can bring home the laundry, get a good meal and take the leftovers.

But it's still a pain sometimes. I had a fight with my dad over a family picnic. It was my uncle's birthday, and the whole family was getting together at a park. I love my uncle, but I had exams coming up. I wound up going because it just wasn't worth the hassle.

Later, I talked to my mom about it. She was on my dad's side, of course, but I think she understood. Things are getting a little better. They still see me as a kid, but they're giving me more space.

EVA

I'm still at home. I suppose I could move out, but it doesn't make sense. This way, I can go to school full time and finish a lot faster. Besides, my parents aren't ready for me to move out. I'm not ready, either.

We're a close family, and I can't imagine being away. I worry sometimes about what it will be like. I'm really kind of dependent, and I don't know how to do a lot of things. It's just easier to let somebody else do it.

I'm in college, and I think I should be growing up more. It's a little scary.

ED

The toughest thing for me has been seeing the same kids I saw in high school. I messed around a lot and got into trouble with the cops a few times. . . nothing too major. It's different now. I know if I don't make it here, it's going to be rough. Besides, I like it ! Can you believe it? I never thought I'd ever like school.

But seeing the same guys from high school is really hard. They see me like I was then. That's how they want me to be.

It's also weird to be in school with old people. I mean some of them are older than my folks. And they know so much! For the first semester, I wouldn't say anything. Now, I do. I found out they're kind of interested in what I'm thinking. I'm really getting into school now, and I'm making some new friends; even have a girlfriend I met here.

WILMA

I came here pretty much knowing that I wanted to be a teacher. I know it's going to take a long time, but I'm determined. I'm getting a good start here; the teachers really lay things out, and they spend time with you if you go see them. I have some friends who transferred from here (to the state university), and they're doing fine. I'm involved in a few activities, too, so it's been good.

Home is something else. My mother just remarried, and my "new dad" and I don't get along. Besides, it's tough to study with my younger brother and sister around. I spend a lot of time at the college. I like it here, and it gets me out of the house.

These four students are quite different from each other, but their life stories reveal some common elements. Each of them believes that college is a time for greater independence and adult responsibility. To some extent, they all feel the need to "break away" from the past and develop a new identity. They may still love their families or see their old friends, but they also recognize that they must establish themselves as separate adults.

Although almost all traditional age college students go through a similar struggle, those attending a community college face an additional hurdle. They must assert their independence while they are still living at or close to home. That makes the process all the more complicated.

But several of the personal narratives provide clues into how community college students approach this challenge. One way is by "negotiating" new roles within the family unit; that is by talking about the demands of college life and trying to come to an agreement over the amount of time that should be devoted to family activities. I don't pretend that this is an easy process. It's not, and it usually takes a while. In most cases, it occurs gradually and requires further discussion and negotiation throughout a person's educational journey.

A second way is by involving oneself in the role of a college student. Establishing an identity within the college is an important step in establishing an identity apart from old routines. It is very important for students 18-21 years of age (and even a little beyond) to attend college events and join college teams, groups, councils or clubs. Through involvement with the college community, people begin to take on a new identity. It affects how they see themselves and how others see them.

The final way is by participating actively in class. It is only natural for people 18-21 to hang back when they find themselves in a class with people old enough to be their parents. I've had students tell me that they could never disagree openly with someone of their parent's generation. Somehow it seemed disrespectful or just not right. In some instances, they also felt that they would be at a disadvantage or not taken seriously.

If you are 18-21, expect to feel a little strange at first. It **is** different to be in a class with people older than yourself. But the feeling of discomfort fades quickly. As people of different generations become accustomed to studying and talking together, they accept the process readily and even enjoy it.

If the truth be known, many students beyond the 18-21 age range believe that **they** are at a disadvantage in going to college with their younger classmates. They may be returning to school after many years and feel that they've gotten too far behind. A forty-five year old man said to me last year, "I doubt if I'll make it. All the kids here grew up with computers, and I can't even turn one on."

Of course, these fears are just as unfounded as the fears of younger students. Students of all ages do well in community colleges, and they benefit greatly from taking classes together. So if you are a traditional age student, don't hang back. Participate actively. You and your classmates will be glad you did.

In summary, the 18-21 year old community college student faces a series of new experiences. At first, the experiences are confusing, but they become more understandable over time. What helps most are patience, involvement in the college, active participation in class and a willingness to work things out at home.

The Student Balancing School, Work or Family Responsibilities

Joan Fine is a student at my school, Three Rivers Community-Technical College. She is also a single mother of two small children. During February, 1994, she was interviewed by Chuck Detmer, a staff writer for the college newspaper. The opening part of Mr. Detmer's article gives an excellent portrayal of the daily challenges confronting many community college students:

61

It's 6:10 a.m. Joan Fine studied until 1:00 a.m. but wasn't able to sleep; her mind is racing to ensure she hasn't forgotten to coordinate anything that might throw off her hectic day's schedule. At 7:00 a.m., she has to wake, feed, bathe and dress her children. She'd like to get them going a little earlier, to make sure her timetable has a little extra leeway, but is reluctant to disturb them. How successful her day will be depends on whether people who have promised to help her run into scheduling problems of their own.

Caring for her two children while attending college has presented Fine with the problem common to most single parents trying to find enough time in a day to do all the things necessary to be both a successful student and a successful parent. Fine's scheduling problems have been magnified by the fact that she has no car and is living on a very limited budget.

Fine, a 29-year-old single parent of two, is attending Three Rivers Community-Technical College with the help of Pell Grants and Job Connection aid, in the hopes of becoming a medical secretary. Becoming self-sufficient and being able to provide for her children, 5-year-old Rebecca and 3-year-old Nicholas, are what keep her motivated. "Being able to give my kids a happy childhood, a good start in life and a college education is what I'm trying to achieve, " said Fine. "It gets tough trying to find the time for school, study and the house without neglecting the kids, but if things work out like I plan, it'll all be worth it."

Hard work, sacrifice and a lot of love and patience are required for a single parent to balance study time with quality time for the children. "It's hard for the kids to understand that Mommy needs time to study," she said. Then after a thoughtful pause, she added, "Studying with endless interruptions is no picnic for Mommy either." Since her divorce, she has had to restructure her life to correspond with everyone else's schedule. She

62

views her divorce as a mixed blessing; " I got rid of a real rat, but lost the freedom that having my own car brought. I have to depend on friends to get me to school, go shopping or take the kids anywhere." Even a little thing like, who will pick up Rebecca, should she become ill at school, required a lot of coordination on Joan's part, not to mention several understanding friends to volunteer their time, cars and phone numbers.

Her typical school days start at 6:30 a.m. which gives her 30 minutes to get herself ready. At 7:00 a.m. she has to get her children up, washed, dressed and fed. At 8:20 a.m. her 5-year-old catches the school bus, and at 8:30 a.m. her youngest is picked up by his baby sitter. Fine takes a bus to the Mohegan campus which leaves at 8:45 a.m.; she's on it and on her way to college provided there have been no glitches in her schedule.

Joan Fine is a strong, organized and motivated person. She is also representative of community college students everywhere who combine college with parenting, a job or both. If you are in this category, rest assured that you are not alone. Most community college students balance the demands of school, work and family. Their lives are not easy, but each year, thousands of them experience the thrill of receiving a diploma.

How do they do it? There is, of course, no single answer to that question. Each individual and each life situation is different. But the story of Joan Fine gives us a useful starting point. The ways that she copes with her daily responsibilities are characteristic of many community college students.

I'm sure you noticed how carefully Ms. Fine schedules her time. She knows to the minute when she must awaken her children and begin the process of getting everyone off to school. The newspaper article points out that she continues to follow a tight schedule throughout the day and evening. Her life lacks spontaneity, but she is able to attend classes, study and tend to her home and children.

63

Of course, she can't do it alone. Like other community college students in her situation, Joan Fine reaches out and asks for help. Until she is able to get a car, her friends drive her to many of the places she needs to go. When she has an emergency, like an ill child, her friends are there as well. Ms. Fine is fortunate to have cooperative friends, but to make everything work, she needs to plan ahead. She has to give people advance notice and iron out backup plans for unusual or emergency situations. If she waits until the last minute, it may be too late.

Although Joan Fine's children are small, they have had to make adjustments too. Since Mommy is on a tight schedule, so are they. She is careful to explain why she needs time to study and ensures that each child receives daily individual attention. She also knows that she will experience interruptions until her children are older. But she is insistent on scheduling study time and sticking to it. This is the only way she can do well in her classes.

Students who are married must also pay attention to family relationships. In addition to their children, they must be concerned about the effect of school on their spouses. The husbands and wives of community college students need to adjust to a new routine and perhaps greater home responsibility as well. To the extent possible, problems should be anticipated and discussed openly.

Finally, if you are a community college student juggling home, work and college, you need to accept what you can't control. Most people in your situation can only attend school part-time, so it takes them longer to complete a degree or certificate. It's important to be realistic and to keep your life in balance. If you become frazzled and exhausted, you'll be cheating yourself and your loved ones. **And** you'll be reducing your chances of completing your education. A student who faces intolerable stress and time pressure over an extended period is more likely to become ill or simply too tired to continue school.

Your best bet is to limit yourself to the number of courses you can handle comfortably. At the beginning, it's difficult to tell what that number is, so be prepared to change. Above all, resist the temptation to overload yourself. Nothing is more discouraging than running from class to class, studying on the run and feeling unprepared for every test.

To do well in college, you must feel well, experience some classroom success and enjoy yourself. Sometimes it's equally important to see a college play or share a cup of coffee with a classmate as it is to study for an exam.

Think back to chapter one. The key point was that the benefits of a community college education occur at every stage of the process, not just at the end. Each semester you enroll, you will develop new abilities, increase your earning power and grow in confidence and self awareness. So catch your breath and take each semester as it comes. The best things in life can't be rushed.

The "First Generation" Student

The "first generation" community college student is the first (or nearly the first) member of his or her family to attend college. Thousands of people fit this description and begin college without knowing what to expect. Even the "front end" process of admissions, placement testing, financial aid and registration can seem strange, impersonal or confusing.

While each situation is different, first generation students often face conflicting expectations. College pulls them in one direction, while their families or friends pull them in another. Howard B. London, Professor of Sociology at Bridgewater State College, recalls a first generation student who took a course in Music Appreciation and tried to play classical music at home. The student reported, "My sister, she really went nuts. There were a couple of friends there, too, having fits. They were looking at me, like "What's the matter with this kid?"

Dr. London goes on to point out that classical music was not really the issue at all. What the student's family and friends actually feared was that she was breaking away, and that they

65

would "lose her." As one person said to her, "We won't be able to talk to you anymore."

At times, the families or friends of first generation students are very proud of them but still worried that college will "change" them. Another student explained to Prof. London:

> *I have sometimes said something that I learned at school, and my mother would shoot me a look. [Imitates his mother:] "My, my, my." But I know she is very, very proud of me. . . [Later] They want me to go on to [a four-year] college from here [a community college], but I know I'm not supposed to become a four-syllable kind of guy. This is not something they would want to see.*

In some cases, the feelings of loved ones go even deeper. Lauri I. Rendón, now an Associate Professor in the Division of Educational Leadership and Policy Studies at Arizona State University, remembers that her decision to attend college was quite difficult for her Mexican American parents to accept:

> *At Laredo Junior College. . . I faced new academic demands and tried to reconcile my new world with my old culture. I know that my mother was feeling angry and frustrated with my tenacious behavior to go to college, although we never really talked about it. It was a subject that was broached in different ways. She would explain that she was tired of being a waitress. She would be irritable that she had to work night shifts in order to sustain the family (my two sisters and me). I knew that for her the ideal daughter would promptly, after graduating from high school, get a job so that her mother would not have to work anymore. Even today I often find myself trying to make up for the fact that I did not fit this ideal vision.*

Not everyone goes through experiences of this kind. But if you are a first generation student, you should be prepared for changes in yourself and, at least, some changes in your relationships with others. As one student said to me, "I have to be careful to tell my folks how much I love them and appreciate them. They know that, but they also see that I'm maybe moving away from them a little bit. I try to reassure them." Another student mentioned that he now has to put up with teasing about being a "college boy." It irritates him sometimes, but he "tries to laugh it off unless it gets out of hand." A third explained to me that she uses "different language" when she's at home and when she's at school. And a fourth recalled that she finally had to "have it out" with a friend who kept giving her "grief about reading all the time."

There are no magic answers. If you are a first generation student, you must look at your individual situation and decide what is workable for you. Of course you should do your best to understand and deal with the concerns and expectations of family and friends. But you also need to be fair to yourself. You may need to "stand your ground" on some issues, even if doing so leads to conflict.

It's always easier to handle difficult situations when you have the support of a friend. Go out of your way to form friendships with fellow students. They can understand what you are going through and offer empathy, encouragement and practical advice.

If you are a first generation student who is also a member of a minority group, college friends are especially important. They reduce the sense of racial or ethnic isolation felt by many minority students on campuses where their numbers are small. For similar reasons, minority students often benefit from participating in college clubs, organizations and activities. A community college can be a warm and inviting place, but it can also be a lonely one.

Conclusion

As chapter five comes to an end, think back for a moment to chapter four. Seek help when you need it. The challenges facing community college students go well beyond the classroom. They involve family relationships, personal priorities and conflicting expectations. Even the strongest students need to "talk things through" once in a while. So don't hold things in. Talk to a counselor, a faculty member or someone else you trust.

NOW, LET'S TALK

I suspect that you have many questions, thoughts and concerns. Now is an excellent time to begin discussing them.

Conversation 1: Talk with the Teacher or Member of the College Staff

What questions or thoughts do you have about your own college at this point?

_____

_____

_____

_____

_____

_____

_____

_____

_____

_____

_____

_____

_____

_____

Conversation 2: Talk with Your Fellow Students

After reading chapter five, what would you like to discuss with new students like yourself? What about students who have attended your college for a while?

_____

_____

_____

_____

_____

_____

_____

Conversation 3: Talk with Friends and Family

This is an important one. Are there any issues or concerns you would like to begin discussing with friends or family members? Think about how you would open each conversation.

_____

_____

_____

_____

_____

_____

_____

Conversation 4: Talk with Yourself

Do you have any additional thoughts or concerns? Do you need more information to move ahead?

_____

_____

_____

_____

_____

_____

_____

Chapter 6

SO, DO IT!

I want your community college education to be fascinating, challenging and satisfying. My wish is that you will awaken each day looking forward to classes, studying, seeing fellow students and participating in campus life. I hope the entire experience gets into your blood.

As you begin the journey, try to keep the following in mind:

✓ **You can do well.** Remember that many community college students succeed even if they disliked or did poorly in school before. A community college education marks a new beginning. It's an opportunity to succeed and enjoy the feelings of accomplishment that come from doing well in the classroom.

✓ **A community college education leads to university transfer, better job opportunities and higher income.** Keep an eye on your final goal. Whether you plan to go on to a university, continue in your present job or start a new career, a community college education will open doors for you.

✓ **The benefits of a community college education occur all along the way, not just at the end.** While the final goal is important, the benefits of a community college education begin immediately and continue throughout the entire process. At every stage, you will become a more self aware, resourceful and fulfilled human being. Perhaps your academic, career or life goals will change, maybe even more than once.

✓ **Determination and patience are rewarded.** You may be one of the fortunate few who begins with a strong academic foundation, no money worries, no family difficulties, no conflicting expectations and no responsibilities beyond going to school. If you are, you are a rare exception. Almost all community college students enter college under conditions that make it harder for them to achieve their educational goals.

And, yet, thousands of them graduate each year. Through determination and patience, they are able to study and work around the obstacles in their way. At times, they have to move slowly, but their persistence pays off in the end.

✓ **Friends make the world go round.** None of us wants to live without friends, but most community college students **can't** live without them. Friends help each other through the rocky moments of college life. Go out of your way to form friendships with your schoolmates. It's often just as important as studying for exams.

✓ **Seeking help is a survival skill.** I've never known a community college student who didn't need help at one time or another. Unfortunately, I've known many who failed to ask for it. Help is available, but you must take the initiative. If you're not sure where to request assistance, ask anyone. Eventually, you'll get the right person. Remember, too, that your fellow students may provide the greatest help of all.

✓ **You have to "get into it."** A community college education is not a grim affair. Sure, there's pressure, and you have to be determined. But you also need to learn enthusiastically and enjoy yourself. Ask questions. Write in the book. Think about what you've read. Exchange ideas. Attend college events. Join college groups. Meet classmates for coffee. Study together. Get into it!

Conclusion

I've been honest with you in this book. I've told you that not every community college student succeeds, and that the problems facing community college students are sometimes difficult to overcome. But I've also told you that thousands of people fulfill their dreams and goals each year. It can be done. So, do it!

NOW, LET'S TALK

Talk with Yourself

For a change, start with your own thoughts and feelings. What are they at this point? What questions do you have as you begin your community college education?

_____

_____

_____

_____

_____

_____

Talk with Others

Remember not to hold things in. Make sure your questions receive answers. Express your concerns to someone with whom you feel comfortable. Make notes on the conversation you want to have.

_____

_____

_____

_____

_____

REFERENCES

CHAPTER 1

The statistics on transfer of community college students to universities appeared in Diana Carter. "Community College Advocates, Educators are not Surprised by University of Michigan Transfer Study." *Community College Week*, October 26, 1992.

Doucette, D., and Rouche, J. E. "Arguments with Which to Combat Elitism and Ignorance about Community Colleges." *Leadership Abstracts*, 1991, 4 (13).

Cetron, M. "An American Renaissance in the Year 2000." *The Futurist* , 1992, 19 (4), 2-11.

The survey of graduating college seniors appeared in Siebert, A., and Walter, T. L. *Student Success: How to Succeed in College and Still Have Time for Your Friends.* Fort Worth, Texas: Harcourt Brace Jovanovich, 1993.

CHAPTER 2

Vest, C. M. "The Sciences and Liberal Arts: Reaching a Common Language." *New Directions for Higher Education* , 1994, (85), 12-20.

Mohrman, K. "The Public Interest in Liberal Education." *New Directions for Higher Education*, 1994, (85), 21-30.

79

CHAPTER 3

Langan, J. *Reading and Study Skills*. New York: McGraw-Hill, 1992.

Siebert, A. and Walter, T. L. *How to Succeed in College and Still Have Time for Your Friends*. Fort Worth, Texas: Harcourt Brace Jovanovich, 1993.

Pellicio, E. Unpublished comments. May, 1994.

CHAPTER 5

Detmer, C. "It's Hard for the Kids to Understand that Mommy Needs Time to Study." *The Current* (college newspaper of Three Rivers Community-Technical College), February, 15, 1994.

London, H. B. "Transformations: Cultural Challenges Faced by First-Generation Students." *New Directions for Community Colleges*, 1992, (80), 5-12.

Rendón, L. I. "From the Barrio to the Academy: Revelations of a Mexican American "Scholarship Girl." *New Directions for Community Colleges*, 1992, (80). 55-64.